Pieces to Play

with

Step by Step

by

Edna Mae Burnam

To my grandson, David Bender

CONTENTS

Book
ISBN 978-1-4234-3594-5

Book/CD
ISBN 978-1-4234-3611-9

WILLIS MUSIC

Exclusively Distributed By

HAL•LEONARD®
CORPORATION
7777 W. BLUEMOUND RD. P.O. BOX 13819 MILWAUKEE, WI 53213

Visit Hal Leonard Online at
www.halleonard.com

TO THE TEACHER

The pieces in this book have been composed to correlate exactly with the Edna Mae Burnam Piano Course STEP BY STEP—Book One. Prefixed to each piece is an indication of the exact page of STEP BY STEP—Book One at which a selection from PIECES TO PLAY may be introduced. When the student reaches this page, he/she is ready to play with ease and understanding.

Rests are omitted in the first four pieces because they are not introduced in STEP BY STEP—Book One until pages 28, 29, and 30. Subsequent pieces do include rests.

All of the pieces in this book may serve as repertoire for the student at this level.

The pieces in this book should be:

1. Perfected;
2. Memorized;
3. Played with expression and poise;
4. Kept in readiness to play for company.

Edna Mae Burnam

MARCH OF THE RADISHES

BY EDNA MAE BURNAM

Moderately fast
Steady and firm

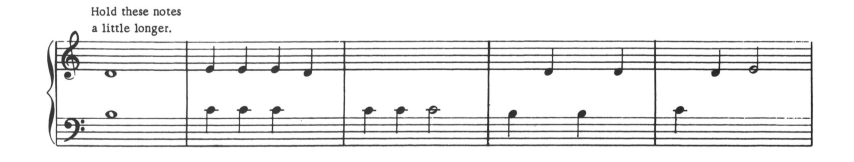

The student is ready to learn this piece when he has reached page 21 of
Edna Mae Burnam's STEP BY STEP - Book One.

A LONELY TUNNEL

BY EDNA MAE BURNAM

Moderately slow
Sad and lonely

medium soft

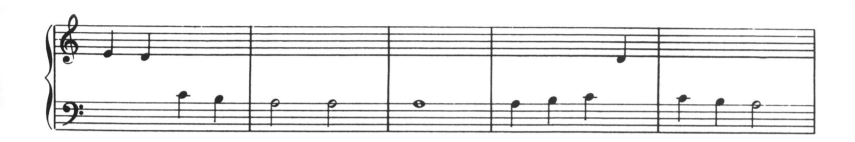

Hold these
notes a little
longer.

very soft

The student is ready to learn this piece when he has reached page 24 of
Edna Mae Burnam's STEP BY STEP – Book One.

SOFT SHADOWS

BY EDNA MAE BURNAM

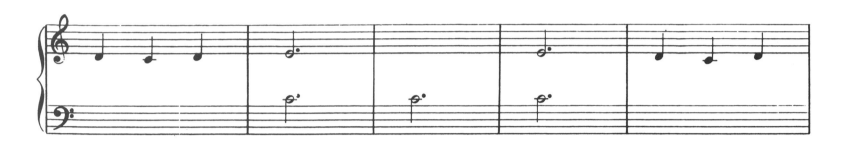

The student is ready to learn this piece when he has reached page 27 of
Edna Mae Burnam's STEP BY STEP – Book One.

A BUMPY STREET

Moderately fast
Louder on the "Bump" notes

BY EDNA MAE BURNAM

The student is ready to learn this piece when he has reached page 30 of
Edna Mae Burnam's STEP BY STEP – Book One.

A CAMEL ON THE DESERT

BY EDNA MAE BURNAM

Moderately slow
Languid

medium soft

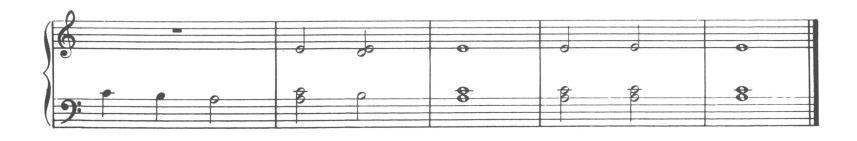

The student is ready to learn this piece when he has reached page 32 of
Edna Mae Burnam's STEP BY STEP – Book One.

SONG IN THE MEADOW

BY EDNA MAE BURNAM

Moderately fast
In a singing style

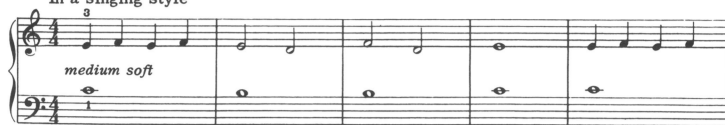

medium soft

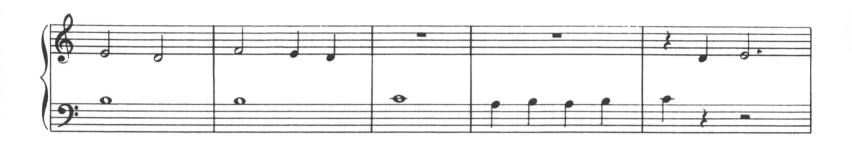

Hold these notes.

slower

The student is ready to learn this piece when he has reached page 34 of
Edna Mae Burnam's STEP BY STEP - Book One.

EVERYBODY MARCH

BY EDNA MAE BURNAM

Play like a march.

medium loud

gradually louder - to the end

loud

*The student is ready to learn this piece when he has reached page 36 of
Edna Mae Burnam's STEP BY STEP – Book One.*

BEACH BALL BOUNCE

BY EDNA MAE BURNAM

Certificate of Merit

This is to certify that

_____

has successfully completed

PIECES TO PLAY

BOOK ONE

BY

EDNA MAE BURNAM

and is now eligible for promotion to

PIECES TO PLAY

BOOK TWO

_____Teacher

Date _____

Edna Mae Burnam

Edna Mae Burnam (1907–2007) is one of the most respected names in piano pedagogy. She began her study of the instrument at age seven with lessons from her mother, and went on to major in piano at the University of Washington and Chico State Teacher's College in Los Angeles. In 1935, she sold "The Clock That Stopped"—one of her original compositions still in print today—to a publisher for $20. In 1937, Burnam began her long and productive association with Florence, Kentucky-based Willis Music, who signed her to her first royalty contract. In 1950, she sent manuscripts to Willis for an innovative piano series comprised of short and concise warm-up exercises—she drew stick figures indicating where the "real" illustrations should be dropped in. That manuscript, along with the original stick figures, became the best-selling *A Dozen a Day* series, which has sold more than 25 million copies worldwide; the stick-figure drawings are now icons.

Burnam followed up on the success of *A Dozen a Day* with her *Step by Step Piano Course*. This method teaches students the rudiments of music in a logical order and manageable pace, for gradual and steady progress. She also composed hundreds of individual songs and pieces, many based on whimsical subjects or her international travels. These simple, yet effective learning tools for children studying piano have retained all their charm and unique qualities, and remain in print today in the Willis catalog. Visit **www.halleonard.com** to browse all available piano music by Edna Mae Burnam.

A DOZEN A DAY

by Edna Mae Burnam

The **Dozen a Day** books are universally recognized as one of the most remarkable technique series on the market for all ages! Each book in this series contains short warm-up exercises to be played at the beginning of each practice session, providing excellent day-to-day training for the student. The audio CD is playable on any CD player and features fabulous backing tracks by Ric Iannone. For Windows® and Mac computer users, the CD is enhanced so you can access MIDI files for each exercise and adjust the tempo.

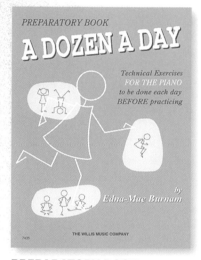

PREPARATORY BOOK
00414222 Book Only $3.95
00406476 Book/CD Pack $8.95
00406479 CD Only $9.95
00406477 Book/GM Disk Pack .. $13.95
00406480 GM Disk Only $9.95

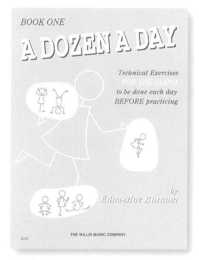

BOOK 1
00413366 Book Only $3.95
00406481 Book/CD Pack $8.95
00406483 CD Only $9.95
00406482 Book/GM Disk Pack .. $13.90
00406484 GM Disk Only $9.95

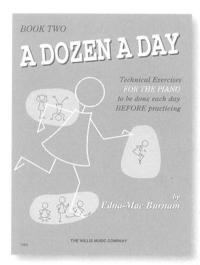

BOOK 2
00413826 Book Only $3.95
00406485 Book/CD Pack $8.95
00406487 CD Only $9.95
00406486 Book/GM Disk Pack .. $13.90
00406488 GM Disk Only $9.95

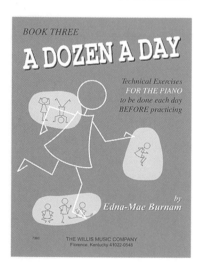

BOOK 3
00414136 Book Only $4.95
00416760 Book/CD Pack $9.95

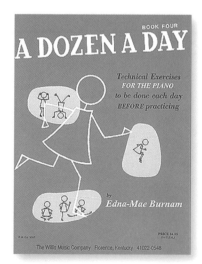

BOOK 4
00415686 Book Only $5.95
00416761 Book/CD Pack $10.95

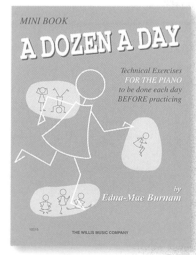

MINI BOOK
00404073 Mini Book $3.95
00406472 Book/CD Pack $8.95
00406474 CD Only $9.95
00406473 Book/GM Disk Pack .. $13.90
00406475 GM Disk Only $9.95

WILLIS MUSIC

EXCLUSIVELY DISTRIBUTED BY
Hal•Leonard®

Prices, contents, and availability subject to change without notice. Prices listed in U.S. funds.

TEACHING LITTLE FINGERS TO PLAY MORE

TEACHING LITTLE FINGERS TO PLAY MORE

by Leigh Kaplan

Teaching Little Fingers to Play More is a fun-filled and colorfully illustrated follow-up book to *Teaching Little Fingers to Play*. This book strengthens skills learned while easing the transition into John Thompson's *Modern Course, First Grade.*

00406137	Book Only	$5.95
00406527	Book/CD Pack	$14.95
00406524	GM Disk Only	$9.95

SUPPLEMENTARY SERIES

All books include optional teacher accompaniments.

CLASSICS
arr. Randall Hartsell
MID-ELEMENTARY LEVEL
7 solos: Marche Slave • Over the Waves • Polovtsian Dance (from the opera *Prince Igor*) • Pomp and Circumstance • Rondeau • Waltz (from the ballet *Sleeping Beauty*) • William Tell Overture.

00406760	Book Only	$5.95
00416513	Book/CD	$15.95
00416435	Book/GM Disk	$15.90

DISNEY TUNES
arr. Glenda Austin
MID-ELEMENTARY LEVEL
9 songs, including: Circle of Life • Colors of the Wind • A Dream Is a Wish Your Heart Makes • A Spoonful of Sugar • Under the Sea • A Whole New World • and more.

00416750	Book Only	$6.95
00416751	Book/CD Pack	$15.95

JAZZ AND ROCK
Eric Baumgartner
MID-ELEMENTARY LEVEL
11 solos, including: Big Bass Boogie • Crescendo Rock • Funky Fingers • Jazz Waltz in G • Rockin' Rhythm • Squirrel Race • and more!

00406765	Book Only	$5.95
00406828	Book/CD Pack	$15.90
00416554	GM Disk Only	$9.95

JEWISH FAVORITES
arr. Eric Baumgartner
MID-ELEMENTARY LEVEL
7 songs: Ani Purim • Hava Nagila • Oyfn Pripetshik • Rozhinkes mit Mandlen • Russian Sher • Siman Tov • Zemer Atik.

00416755	Book Only	$5.95
00416756	Book/CD Pack	$15.95

RECITAL PIECES
by Carolyn Miller
MID-ELEMENTARY LEVEL
6 solos: The Boatman • Happy Day • It's Cool • Let's Rock • Mystery • Recital Waltz.

00416540	Book Only	$5.95
00416677	Book/CD Pack	$15.95

SONGS FROM MANY LANDS
arr. Carolyn C. Setliff
MID-ELEMENTARY LEVEL
7 solos: Ach, Du Lieber Augustin • The Ash Grove • Au Clair de la Lune • Mexican Hat Dance • My Bonnie • Tarantella • That's an Irish Lullaby.

00416688	Book Only	$5.95
00416689	Book/CD Pack	$15.95

Also available:

AMERICAN TUNES
arr. Eric Baumgartner
MID-ELEMENTARY LEVEL

00406755	Book Only	$5.95
00406820	Book/CD Pack	$15.90
00406822	CD Only	$9.95
00406819	Book/GM Disk	$15.90
00416542	GM Disk Only	$9.95

BLUES AND BOOGIE
Carolyn Miller
MID-ELEMENTARY LEVEL

00406764	Book Only	$5.95
00416512	Book/CD Pack	$15.90
00416562	CD Only	$9.95
00406825	Book/GM Disk	$15.90
00416561	GM Disk Only	$9.95

CHRISTMAS CAROLS
arr. Carolyn Miller
MID-ELEMENTARY LEVEL

00406763	Book Only	$5.95
00416475	Book/CD Pack	$15.95
00416556	GM Disk Only	$9.95

CHRISTMAS FAVORITES
arr. Eric Baumgartner
MID-ELEMENTARY LEVEL

00416723	Book Only	$6.95
00416724	Book/CD Pack	$15.95

FAMILIAR TUNES
arr. Glenda Austin
MID-ELEMENTARY LEVEL

00406761	Book Only	$5.95
00416484	Book/CD Pack	$15.90
00416436	Book/GM Disk	$15.90
00416541	GM Disk Only	$9.95

HYMNS
arr. Glenda Austin
MID-ELEMENTARY LEVEL

00406762	Book Only	$5.95
00416485	Book/CD Pack	$15.90

Prices, contents, and availability subject to change without notice.

WILLIS MUSIC

HAL•LEONARD®
CORPORATION
7777 W. BLUEMOUND RD. P.O. BOX 13819
MILWAUKEE, WISCONSIN 53213

EXCLUSIVELY DISTRIBUTED BY

Complete song lists online at
www.halleonard.com

Disney characters and artwork
are © Disney Enterprises, Inc.

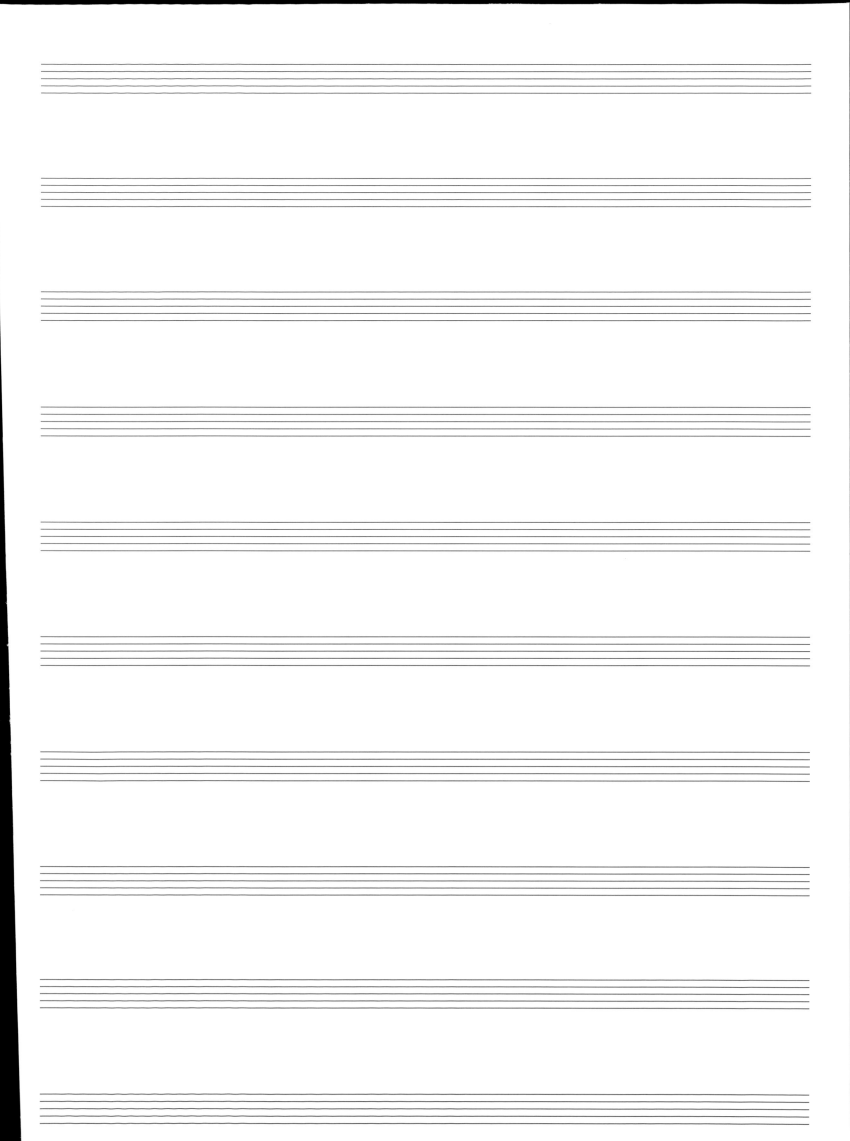